# Totally Useless

# Office Skills

*Other books by Rick Davis:*

Totally Useless Skills
Totally Useless Skills for Kids


*Videos by Rick Davis:*

Totally Useless Skills
Totally Useless Office Skills

# Totally Useless
# Office Skills

**by Rick Davis**

**HOBBLEBUSH BOOKS**

PUBLISHED BY HOBBLEBUSH BOOKS

Brookline, NH 03033

Library of Congress Catalog Card Number: 96-78425

ISBN 0-9636413-2-8

Copyright © 1996 by Rick Davis

Printed in the United States of America

8   7   6   5   4   3   2   1

To contact the author, write: The Institute of Totally Useless Skills, P.O. Box 181, Temple, NH 03084.
To contact publisher, write: Hobblebush Books,
17-A Old Milford Rd., Brookline, NH 03033.

# Dedication

*This book is dedicated to you, for helping me make a living.**

*\* Outside of the office.*

# Acknowledgments

Spirit: Hart, my dad

Designer, computer genius,
poet, and publisher: Sidney Hall, Jr.

Photo Credits: Gary Richardson – pages XII, 2, 3, 8, 9, 15, 16, 17, 23, 24, 25, 27, 29, 31, 43, 51, 55, 57, 61, 63-66, 72, 74-77, 79, 81, 86, 99, 103-105
Phebe Lewan – pages 5, 10, 12, 14, 19, 20, 22, 32, 50, 53, 60, 62, 67-69, 80, 88, 91, 94, 95, 96
Mark Corliss – pages 58, 98, 100, 107
Bruce Taylor – pages 44, 47

Illustrations: Gene Mater – pages 30, 37, 38, 39, 46, 52, 82, 84.
All other illustrations are by Rick Davis.

Editing: Sidney Hall, Jr., Kim and Judy Gilliland, Tim Clarke, Jackie Davis, Ray Sweeney, Nina Eppes, Nancy Davis

Wifely tolerance. Jackie Davis

Fantastic human beings: Nancy Davis, Pat Burke, Rita Rosekranz, Emily Hall, Mr. Stowe, Dawn Christensen, Steve Brown, Tom Richards

Models: Laura Campbell, Putnam Ercoline, Rick Smily, Mark Stone, Glory B. Luebbermann, Brian High, Tammy Grenier, June Sheldon

People who taught me skills: Lee Faulkner (Business Card Animals), Mike Perry (Flying Memos), Jim Cook (Telepathic Secretary), Diane Ward (Desk Monster), Murray Backer (All Tied Up), Chris Yerlig (Instant Printed Business Card)

# Contents

## Modern Technology

## Your Amazing Business Card

## Totally Useless Things To Do At Your Desk

## Totally Useless Pencil Tricks

## Totally Useless Paper Stunts

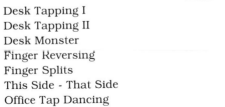

# Preface

*Writing prefaces might, itself, be called a useless skill, since no one ever reads them.*

*Except, apparently, you. So, let's skip this part, shall we, and move right along to something else you don't need to read...*

# Introduction

Hello and welcome to *Totally Useless Office Skills*, the book that none of you have been waiting for.

What you have just stumbled upon is a training manual that will show you how to enhance your work environment through the judicious elimination of production.

Inside you'll find pencil tricks, paper stunts, calculator games, phone songs, and more. In short, it's everything you'll never need to know.

No doubt you are already familiar with many useless office skills such as: understanding your computer, getting along with your supervisor, and that perennial favorite – job security. But with this book, you will go boldly where no one has gone before. (At least no one interested in advancing past middle management.)

I called this book *Useless Skills* for a very important reason. If I called it *UseFUL Skills*, no one would buy it.

But actually, you'll find these skills *can* be very useful. They can serve as antidotes to occupational stress. They can help you network. And, at the very least, they can be a good way to waste time.

At company expense.

# Modern Technology

*Think of all the complex high-tech skills necessary to succeed in today's business world: telecommunication, document management, spreadsheet analysis, Nintendo. The trouble is, there's not enough time to learn EVERYTHING. So, it becomes extremely important to distinguish between skills which are necessary to know, and skills which are NOT necessary to know...*

*Like the following...*

# The Endless Fax

*This stunt is guaranteed to not make you Employee of the Month, you'll be greatly relieved to know.*

Make two copies of a nice friendly message, like...

Tape them together. Feed them to your fax machine and start sending. When the first sheet comes out, quickly tape it to the second sheet to form a loop.

*Now go on a long vacation. See if anything interesting happens by the time you get back.*

# The Long Fax

*You can make an extremely good living being totally useless. Just look at our members of Congress. Or perhaps you'll find the following a bit more palatable.*

As your fax is being fed, hold it with a slight tension so that it feeds slower. As a result, your fax will come out looking like this.

To understand it, the mildly (repeat mildly) amused receiver must read your fax at an extremely oblique angle.

*Think of it as corporate upsizing.*

# Close Encounters with Your Copy Machine

Everyone knows that you can photocopy various parts of your body, like your hand …

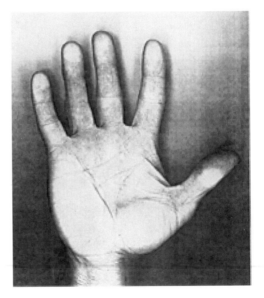

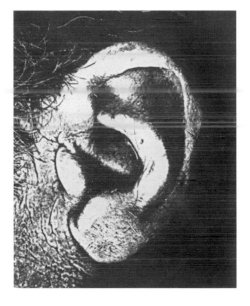

your ear...

...and this other well known part of your anatomy  ➜ ➜

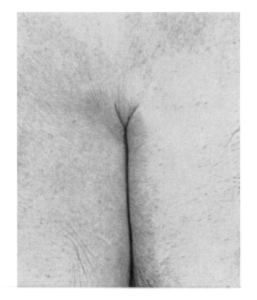

... your armpit.

# How to Tear a Phone Book in Half

*Here's your chance to express your warm feelings about the phone company.*

**1)** Hold the phone book against your torso like this. Notice how the page edges are not even, but staggered.

**2)** Make a one inch tear right down the middle of the book. This is not as difficult as it sounds because, due to the staggered paper edges, you're not ripping all the pages at the same time.

**3)** Turn the book over and repeat this action. You'll wind up with one tear about 2 inches long.

**4)** Now hold the book very close to the tear. Move your right hand *down and to the left*, and move your left hand *up and to the right*. Then reverse directions. Going back and forth like this you'll eventually rip the phone book in half.

*...sometime this fiscal year.*

# Software Balancing

*To execute this program, run...*
**A:SETUP.EXE**
*Then run...*
**A:PICKUP.EXE**

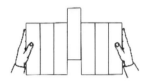

**1)** Pick up 7 software boxes like this.

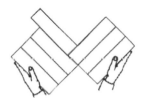

**2)** Slightly press boxes together while curling hands underneath, to get this.

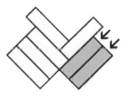

**3)** Move shaded boxes into this position.

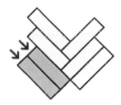

**4)** Ditto.

**5)** Move bottom right hand box into this position.

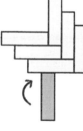

**6)** Turn bottom left hand box.

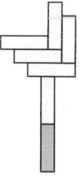

**7)** Bottom right hand box goes underneath.

# Hardware Balancing

You are here

# Your Amazing Business Card

*Are you always getting caught without your business card? Here are some ways to make sure this will happen more often...*

# Quarter Balancing

*A recent survey has shown that 40% of every workday is spent doing things which accomplish absolutely nothing. These include activities like coffee breaks, phone tag, and committee meetings. So, if you are not accomplishing anything anyway, why not do it with style? Like so...*

Fold a business card in half so it forms a 'V'. Stand it on edge on a table. Lay a quarter over the point of the 'V'.

Grab the ends of the card, and *slowly* pull them apart so the card becomes straight. The quarter will balance on the edge of the card.

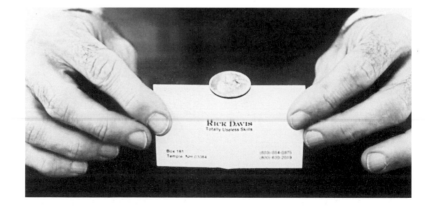

14

# The Sticking Business Card

*The life of an office worker is not pretty. But when the going gets tough, the tough, of course, take a sick day. Or they do this...*

Ask a co-worker to hold a business card against the wall, and then let go. Of course, the card will fall. But, amazingly, when *you* do the same thing, *the card sticks to the wall.*

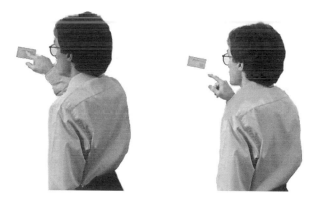

**THE SECRET**: Rub your shoes on the rug before going to the wall. Static electricity will do the rest.

# The Disappearing Business Card

*Usually, people do unto your card exactly what you do unto theirs. They throw it out. But now, with this technique, you can make your card disappear before they do.*

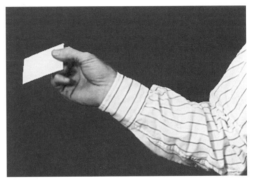

1) Hold a business card like this.

2) Now push forward with your thumb while curling your fingers inward toward your palm. The card will flip over to the back of your hand, like this.

For
The Appearing
Business Card,
do the reverse.

 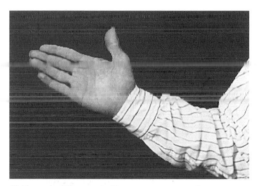

**3)** Grab 2 corners using your pinky and first finger.

**4)** Keep holding on to those corners, and open your hand. PRESTO, your card has disappeared.

Keep your hand relaxed and grab the corners so they don't show when you open your hand. Also, you should mask this entire maneuver by moving your hand *down* on Step 2 and 3, and then *up* on step 4.

*This could be the beginning of a whole new career, which is a good thing, because it might be the end of your old career.*

# The Mysterious Business Card Cut

*Notice something funny about this figure? It seems to be a drawing of something that could not possibly exist. But it can. Here's how..*

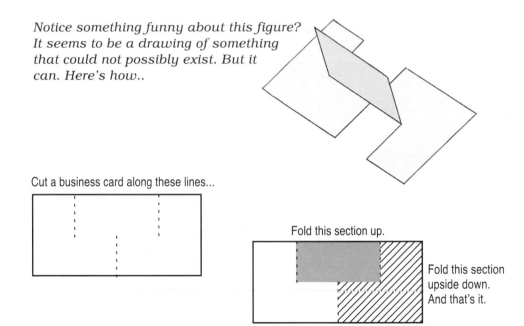

Cut a business card along these lines...

Fold this section up.

Fold this section upside down. And that's it.

*Now for the sadistic part. Challenge a co-worker to make the same thing.*

# Instant Printed Business Card

*...Need business cards printed in a hurry? Here's how...*

**1)** Hold your business card, blank side up, in this position:

**2)** Simultaneously, *move your thumb under the card*, grab the card between thumb and 1st finger, and turn your hand over to arrive at this

Due to your incredible deftness, it will *appear* that you've turned the card over, but you haven't (I hope). Notice the hand has turned over *and* moved from right to left.

**3)** Now make a fist, holding the card inside with its printed side *up*. With your opposite hand, start tapping on the top of your hand (like you're typing on a keyboard). As you do this, slowly push the card with your thumb so that it gradually appears (as if it's being printed).

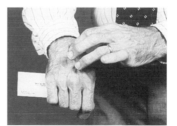

*Now you're in business.*

19

# Business Card Animals

*Stressed out? Try this. It's cheaper than therapy.*

Fold your business card.

Cut as shown.
Then fold neck up.

Unfold and reverse the fold
between the large dots…

…so it looks like this.

Fold as shown, then
unfold and reverse
between the dots.

Make small cuts on
these dotted lines.
Don't cut the fold.

Perk ears up.
Poke tail in.

20

Using the basic pattern on the previous page, you can create all these creatures by simply lengthening or shortening body parts.

21

# Head Through a Business Card

*It's a well known fact that 90% of our brain power is not utilized...as clearly evidenced by the following.*

First, bet a co-worker (the gullible type) that you can put your head through a business card.

**1)** Fold and cut a card as shown. Don't cut all the way through.

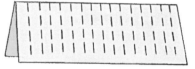

**2)** Turn it over and cut between the original cuts, exactly as shown.

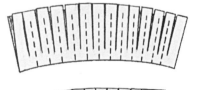

**3)** Unfold the card, and cut as shown. Notice that you don't cut the card all the way to the edges, because you would be cutting it in half.

Start here.

End here.

Now spread it open, stick your astounded head through it, and collect your bet.

*Using the same method you can: stick your body through an index card; stick yourself and a friend through a piece of paper; or, something you've always wanted to do, drive your car through a newspaper.*

# Totally Useless Things To Do At Your Desk

*Useless Office Skills improve desk efficiency! Consider...*

*If you do 3 things at once, you'll do none of them well. If you do 2 things at once, you'll do better. And if you do just 1 thing, you'll do better still. Therefore, to achieve maximum efficiency, do nothing at all.*

*Here are some excellent suggestions for how to do precisely that...*

# Post-It™ Poses

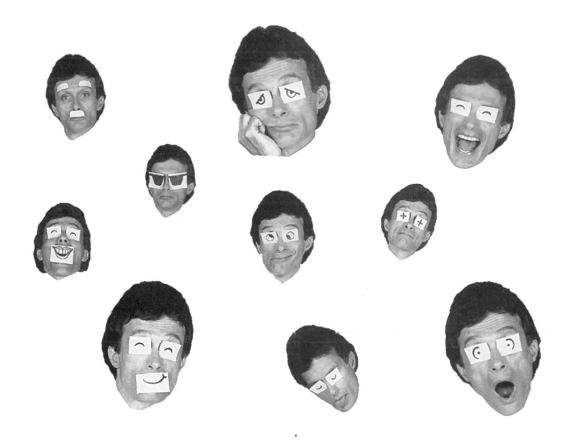

*TOTALLY*
*USELESS*
*THINGS*
*TO DO*
*AT YOUR*
*DESK*

# Death Defying Letter Opener Swallowing

*I hate lawsuits. So please study the last photo extremely carefully...*

*...and remember kids, you CAN do this at home. In fact, in light of the recent rash of corporate layoffs, perhaps you should do this only at home.*

27

# Marker Top Whistling

*Blow air directly over a marker top, and you're sure to get everyone's attention...*

*...and possibly a sexual harassment suit.*

# The Invisible Elevator

TOTALLY
USELESS
THINGS
TO DO
AT YOUR
DESK

*Be sure to tell your therapist you're doing this on purpose.*

TIPS:
- Deadpan look
- Vertical spine
- Don't look down.

**1)** Stand behind a desk.
**2)** Pretend to punch an elevator button.
**3)** Do a very subtle upward bounce (as if the initial movement of the elevator jolted you a little).
**4)** *Slowly and steadily* bend your knees and "descend" behind the desk.

To come back up, reverse the steps, and end with a little jolt to show that the elevator has stopped.

*You can also do the Invisible Stairs, the Invisible Escalator, and – the next time you are laid off – the Invisible Trap Door.*

# How To Bounce a Jar of Rubber Cement

**1)** Gather up co-workers who look like they could use some mild amusement, and ask them "Did you know that jars of rubber cement can bounce off the floor?" Then, after the ensuing long silence...

**2)** Sit at a desk, so that your lower body can't be seen (unlike this photograph). Face to the side, and hold a jar of rubber cement over your head. Make sure everyone else is on the opposite side of the desk.

**3)** Bring your arm sharply down as if you were going to throw the jar at your feet. The arm is now perpendicular to the floor, pointing down. Now comes the tricky part...

*TOTALLY*
*USELESS*
*THINGS*
*TO DO*
*AT YOUR*
*DESK*

**4)** Instead of throwing the jar down to the floor, throw it *up*. But you must throw it up in a special way. *Keep your hand and forearm hidden BELOW the table level.*

**5)** Now for another tricky part. At the precise moment that the jar would have left your hand had you actually thrown it at the floor, *tap the floor with your foot*. This provides a substitute sound that completes the illusion of the jar hitting the floor. Throw the jar a split second after you tap your foot. Now, one more subtle touch…

**6)** Don't move your arm to catch the jar until the jar reaches the top of its flight. Keep that upper arm motionless and the forearm *below* the table level. Wait for the jar to reach its apex. Then catch the jar on its way down. It's only a split second delay, but it's crucial to complete the illusion.

# Multiple Rubber Band Shooting

*Guaranteed to expand, so to speak, your rubber band pleasure.*

Hold your right hand palm up. Loop 5 rubber bands over the tips of your right fingers.

Now, with your left hand palm down, put the tips of your left fingers through the rubber bands.

*...a great way to break the ice at your next tax audit.*

TOTALLY
USELESS
THINGS
TO DO
AT YOUR
DESK

# Jumping Rubber Bands

*Magic, anyone?*

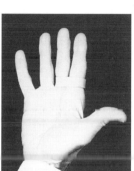

**1)** Loop rubber band around first 2 fingers.

**2)** Lift this loop up and place all four fingers through it so the rubber band rests on your finger nails.

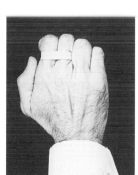

**3)** Turn your hand over and you will see this.

**4)** Now say those well-known magic words, *"Three Day Weekend,"* and quickly open your hand. The rubber band will "magically" jump.

*More impressive...* If you start with two rubber bands (one starting around fingers 1 and 2, and one starting around fingers 3 and 4), the two bands will switch places.

# The Rubber Band Ball

*I want you to take a long look at this — because
I wasted a lot of rubber bands making it.*

# Mystery in the Middle

TOTALLY
USELESS
THINGS
TO DO
AT YOUR
DESK

Hold a ruler on your hands, as shown in this picture. You may put your hands at any two points. Now bring your palms together, slowly. *Amazingly your hands will always end up under the exact midpoint.* If you try to separate your hands, one hand will move, but the other will always stay

*Anyone can do this trick – even with Carpal-Tunnel.*

# The Linking Paper Clips

*It takes a certain mind, or lack of one, to do the following.*

Duplicate this setup exactly. Grab **A** with one hand and **B** with the other. Now, pull!

*The clips will mysteriously link together.*

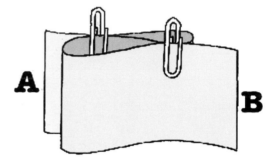

Now for something more impressive. Fold the paper like this:

Here's the top view. Place clips at these dots so that their short loops are facing away from you. Pull the ends of the bill and — voila! — *four linked paper clips.*

TOTALLY
USELESS
THINGS
TO DO
AT YOUR
DESK

# 31 Paper Clips

*Here is one of those annoying little games that are rigged in such a way that YOU always win.*

Only two people can play. On each turn, a player can choose to pick up either 1, 2, 3, 4, 5, or 6 clips, but no more. The object of the game is to *not* pick up the last clip. If you know the secret, you can win every time.

**THE SECRET:** Be sure to pick up the 9th, 16th, and 23rd clip.

*In other words: pick your clips by clipping your picks.*

# Totally Useless Pencil Tricks

*Forget computers. Without PENCILS, civilization as we know it would come to an abrupt end. And when civilization comes to an end, that's when the fun begins, as in the following...*

# Floating Pencil I

*Just think how much you will impress your supervisor when you execute this important job skill.*

*Just don't show how you did it.*

# Floating Pencil II

*...by the same folks who brought you Floating Pencil I.*

**1)** Hold a pencil eraser between your thumbs, with the pencil pointing at the floor.

**2)** Fold your 3rd fingers inward.

**3)** Interlock the rest of your fingers, keeping your 3rd fingers back.

**4)** Still holding the pencil top with your thumbs, grab the pencil with the pads of your 3rd fingers. Then let go with your thumbs, and show off your "floating" pencil.

Move it around with your fingers

42

# Magnetic Pencils

Press two pencil erasers together.  Count to twenty.

When you try to slowly move them away from each other,
they will feel for a moment as if they were magnetized.

*(I didn't say these were good tricks - just useless ones.)*

# Rubber Pencil

*...a classic useless office skill.*

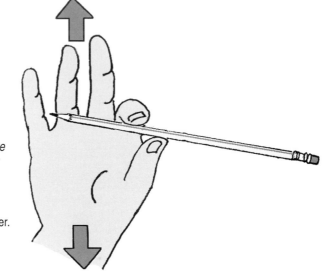

Hold a pencil 1/3 of its length away from its tip.

*Hold it loosely, and DON'T move your fingers.* Rather, move your whole *arm* up and down.

With the proper frequency, the pencil appears to turn into rubber.

*The pencil appears to be rubber due to a phenomenon called retinal persistence. Your ego appears to be enlarged due to a phenomenon called instant talent.*

# Mysterious Pencil Lift

Try lifting a pencil exactly as shown

Note: The 1st and 3rd fingers are not under the pencil, but *just touch the side of the pencil.*

To do this, you need a pencil with ridges. Spread your fingers as wide as possible, then approach the pencil straight down. Jam the ridges of the pencil between the fingernail and the flesh of your 1st and 3rd fingers. Reach over as far as possible with your 2nd finger. Lift.

*..also known as creative pencil pushing.*

45

# Split Pencil

*Used to be, a worker had to work 12 hours a day. Then it was 8. Experts predict that, soon, workers will only need to work 2 hours a day. With a trend like this, workers eventually will not have to work at all. Here's an excellent suggestion for how to do just that...*

Hold a pencil, as shown, at eye level. Look at something far away. Rub your palms together, slowly.

*The pencil will look like it's splitting in front of your eyes.*

# The Disappearing Pencil

**1)** Touch your palm with a pencil eraser and say "One".

**2)** Touch your palm with the pencil a second time and say, "Two".

**Tips:**
- Look at your empty hand, *not* the pencil.
- Hide your ear from your audience. (Duh!)

**3)** Move the pencil behind your ear, and *leave it there.*

**4)** With your now empty hand, *pretend to touch* your palm with a pencil a third time and say "THREE!"

*Of course, you don't really need to make your pencil disappear. You can count on co-workers to do it for you.*

# Thumbs on Top; Thumbs on Bottom

*...yet another way to enjoy yourself by confusing those around you.*

**The CHALLENGE:**

go from this...                    ...to this...                    ...and then back to this...

*...without letting go of the pencil or touching either end.*

48

# Here's how it's done, (if you insist)...

1) Start with the eraser on your left.

2) Make an "X" with your thumbs, right over left.

3) The fingers of the right hand reach between the thumb and fingers of the left hand, and grab the eraser.

4) Your right fingers then pull the eraser end to the right, while simultaneously, your left thumb pulls the other end to the left.

# To reverse:

1) Again make an "X" with your thumbs. This time right under left, so that left thumb is between right thumb and pencil.

2) Right fingers reach between left thumb and left fingers, and touch base of left palm. At this point, make sure left thumb and right first finger are *under* the pencil.

3) Push eraser end *up* with left thumb, and you will reach the original position.

# Twirling Pencil

*...a time-honored, time-killing technique.*

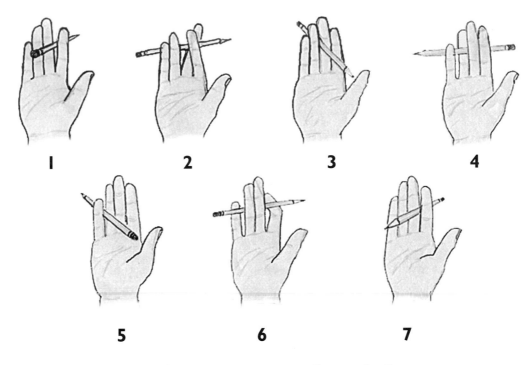

*Do this with a pointer and your presentations will never be the same.*

# Two Pencils

*Office life is filled with weird feelings, such as the sensory loss you feel as your pointed shoes gradually cut off your circulation, the anatomical phenomenon known to all-day-sitters as flat butt, and the peculiar sense of dampness one feels at the mention of the word 'audit'. Here's one more for the road.*

Have a friend close his or her eyes and cross these two fingers...

Now take a pencil and gently rub the eraser forward and back between the fingers. Be sure to touch both fingers at the same time.

It will feel like two pencils!

*Important: it won't work if you do this to yourself. You need a friend – preferably one that is not embarrassed about rubbing you in public.*

# Totally Useless Paper Stunts

*In grade school, it was spit balls. In junior high it was paper airplanes. And in high school, it was passing notes. But now that you've firmly established yourself in the grown-up business world, it's time for something really mindless, like the following...*

# Balancing the Books

*Unlike me, this trick really works.*

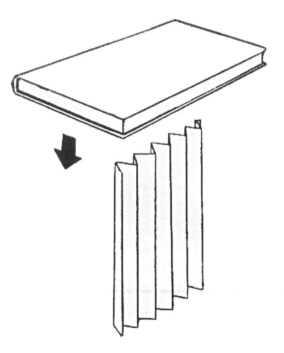

*...just don't do this with the Oxford Unabridged Hernia Inducing Dictionary.*

# Paper Balancing

*Need to work up the latest balance sheet? No problem...*

Pinch two corners of your paper as shown. As you pinch, gently pull the corners in opposite directions.

Place one of the folded corners on the tip of your finger. Raise your hand to about shoulder level. Look at the top of the paper, not the bottom. And balance away!

*Someone should tell our government about this.*

# Flying Fishes

*This stunt is so easy, you can do it even if you don't know how to do it, or even why you're doing it. For that matter, it's probably best if you don't ever consider why you're doing it.*

Cut a strip of paper 1/2" x 4". Cut two slits as shown, then insert one slit into the other.

Hold this figure at the 'X', raise it above your head, make sure no one important is looking, and let go. See what happens.

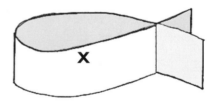

*...a cheap – definitely cheap – thrill.*

# Helicopter

*Here's something to do with your next paycheck. You'll have to rip it up, but if
you've ever dealt with the I.R.S., you should be used to that.*

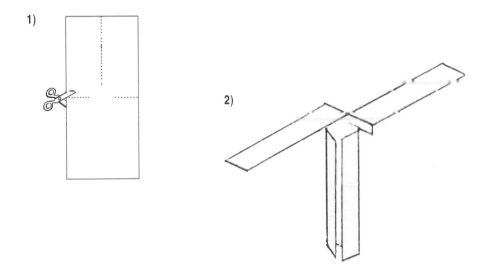

*Hold this contraption over your head and drop it into a recycling bin.*

# Hole in Your Boss's Head

*This trick is so easy, even I can do it...*

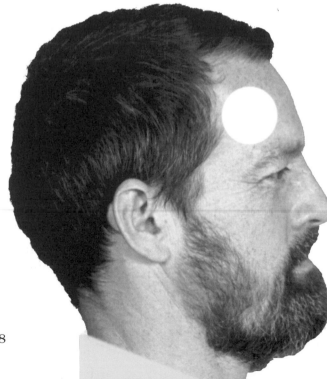

Roll up a piece of paper into a tube. Hold this tube against your boss's forehead like this.

Look through this tube with your right eye, from your boss's right. Keep both eyes open. *You'll see a hole in your boss's head.* *

\* *...the one you've always known was there.*

# Office Boomerang

Cut this shape out of an index card. A rough estimate will do, but make one end longer. Place it on the top of your left fist. Flick it off by hitting one end with your right 1st finger.

*Q*uestion: *Why are boomerangs like office workers?*

*A*nswer: *They keep coming back – for no apparent reason.*

59

# Flying Memos

*This will take you 15 minutes. 1 minute to fold it, 1 minute to fly it, and 13 minutes to get it out of the overhead lighting.*

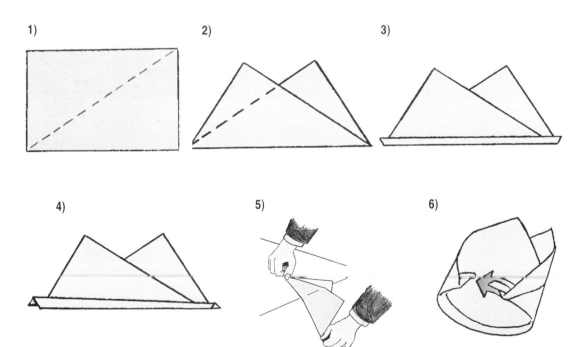

1)

2)

3)

4)

5)

6)

*"Here's that confidential file you wanted, boss!"*

# Pushing Your Buttons

*Why do we work? We work to make money.*

*Why do we make money? So we can buy things.*

*Why do we buy things? So we don't have to work to make these things.*

*Therefore, the ultimate goal of working is to not work at all.*

*As in the following...*

# Pixel Puzzles

*This is for those of you who like cute little puzzles. All seven of you.*

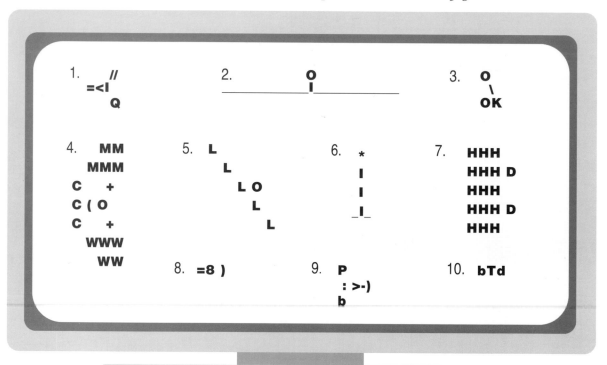

1.
```
     //
=<I
   Q
```

2.
```
              O
_____I_____
```

3.
```
O
 \
  OK
```

4.
```
   MM
  MMM
C   +
C ( O
C   +
  WWW
  WW
```

5.
```
L
  L
    L O
      L
        L
```

6.
```
 *
 I
 I
_I_
```

7.
```
HHH
HHH D
HHH
HHH D
HHH
```

8. `=8 )`

9.
```
P
: >-)
b
```

10. `bTd`

**Answers: 1.** Bird *(look sideways from left)* **2.** Periscope **3.** Kid holding balloon *(look sideways from right)* **4.** Clown *(look sideways from left)* **5.** Ball bouncing down steps **6.** Candle **7.** Truck carrying I-beams *(look from right)* **8.** Nerd with glasses *(look from right)* **9.** Friendly dog *(look sideways from right)* **10.** Side view of diner booth

# Telephone Songs

*This is for frustrated musicians who want us to be frustrated listeners.*

Did you know you can play music on your phone? Just press the buttons on the top (*1,2,3*), and along the right side (*6,9,#*)...

...but don't play the 4,5,7,8,* or 0. They sound even worse than the others.

### Happy Birthday
112163, 112196
11#9632, #9#696

### Louie, Louie
111-66-999-66

### Auld Lang Syne
11113212, 311390
09331212, 310091

### Frère Jacques
1231,1231
369,369
999631, 999631
191,191

### Mary Had a Little Lamb
3212333
222,399
3212333
322321

### Help
911
911
911
911

69

# The Telepathic Secretary

*This is the second best phone trick ever. What's the best? Reaching people when they are in.*

**The trick:** You ask a co-worker to tell you an arbitrary appointment date and hour. Then you call a mysterious "telepathic secretary" on the telephone, and, amazingly, this mysterious secretary instantly tells your visitor the chosen date and time.

**How it's done:**

The secret is that the "telepathic secretary" is an *accomplice* with whom you have secretly worked out a scheme of clues.

Say, for instance, the chosen appointment is June 10, 2 o'clock. Call your accomplice and say:

> *"Hello, could I speak to Ms. Terry?"*

This is not a real name. It is a *secret prompt*. When your accomplice hears this, he or she should *start reciting the months of the year.* (Because you are on the phone, *you* hear this, but the person being tricked does not.) When your accomplice reaches the correct month (which in our example is June), you cut in and say:

> *"Hi, this is (say your name)."*

By cutting in at the precise moment that your accomplice says "June," you are secretly cluing your accomplice that the correct month is June, *and* you are secretly prompting your accomplice to *start counting from 1 to 31*. When your accomplice reaches the correct number (which in our example is 10), cut in with these words:

*"Hello, what is the appointment I just made?"*

Cutting in at this precise moment tips off your accomplice that the correct date is the 10th. It also serves as a prompt for your accomplice to *start counting from 1 to 12* (the hours on a clock). When your accomplice reaches the correct number (which in our example is 2) cut in with these words:

*"Thank you."*

Your accomplice now knows the correct hour, month, and date. So, hand the phone to your visitor, and then your accomplice can complete the act by saying, in an appropriately mysterious tone of voice:

*"The appointment is for June 10th at 2 o'clock."*

# Calculator Words

*Got a calculator? Ask the following questions and then punch out the calculations to get the answer. (Oh, and incidentally, turn the calculator upside down.)*

What will your profit and loss statement look like if you do nothing but Totally Useless Office Skills?
*ANSWER: (5 x 1000) + 500 + 7*

What do you say when the value of your stock goes down 80%?
*ANSWER: (32 x 241) + 22*

In what business are crude statements desirable?
*ANSWER: 1420 ÷ 4 x 2*

If you and your boss get into an argument, what is your wisest course of action?
*ANSWER: 501 X 7*

What is the most common excuse for missing work?
*ANSWER: (77 x 50 ÷ 5) + 1*

If you don't have this excuse, what must you do?
*ANSWER: (64 x 5) – 3*

# Twenty-Five

*This is a game for two people, one calculator, and one coffee break.*

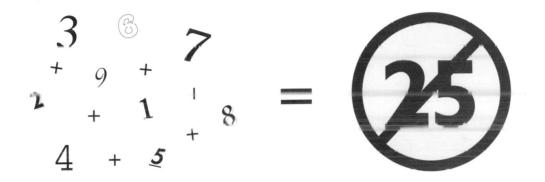

The object is to avoid reaching 25 or higher. Play starts with player #1 entering a 1 digit number on a calculator. Then player #2 adds a 1 digit number to the first number, but it *must be a different number than the one player #1 used*. Play continues as each player in turn adds a *different* number. Once a number has been used, it cannot be used again. It helps to write down the used numbers. The winner is the player who forces the other player to reach or pass 25.

*...or the one who refuses to let go of your neck.*

73

# Disk Shuffle

*Call this the modern equivalent of paper pushing.*

To do this puzzle you will need 5 computer disks. Arrange four disks as shown in A. The challenge is to convert 'A' to 'B' in only 4 moves.

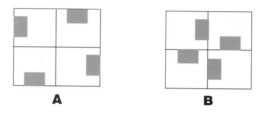

**A**     **B**

A move is made using the fifth disk (the "free disk"). It is used to simultaneously push any 2 disks. In so doing, it replaces the first disk and causes the second disk to become the new free disk. You can orient the free disk so that its shutter is *up* ▪, *down* ▪, *left* ▪, or *right* ▪. You can push in any direction, but each of the four moves must be in a *different* direction. For example…

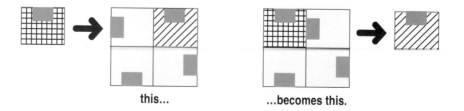

this…          …becomes this.

*Go immediately to the answer on page 110 before you waste any time actually thinking.*

# Push Button Poker

*Now that you've bought that high-power shirt, here's how you can lose it.*

First, deal the "cards." All players have calculators with which they multiply their zip codes by the zip code of another player (or they can multiply random 5 digit numbers). The result will be a 7–10 digit number. The 5 digits on the right constitute your "hand."

*Five-of-a-kind* (like 77777)
beats a *Flush* (like 40628),
which beats *Four-of-a-kind*,
which beats a *Full House* (like 55544),
which beats *Three-of-a-kind*,
which beats *2 Pairs*,
which beats *1 Pair…*

*…which beats working.*

# Things To Do When Put On Hold

*ring...ring...ring...*

*Hello and welcome to the Institute of Totally Useless Skills.*

*If you have a touch-tone phone... press 1.*

*If you don't want to press 1... press 1.*

*If you think it's stupid to press 1... press 1.*

*If you hate automated answering systems which don't put you on hold immediately, but first make you press 12 buttons and THEN put you on hold... press 1 through 12.*

*If you have fantasies concerning marmalade and camels... press 911.*

*And if you are put on hold and you need something to do while you're listening to all that LOOOVELY music... turn the page.*

# Desk Tapping I

*When put on hold, the first inclination many people have is to extract something from their nose. When caught in the act, this maneuver may have certain, shall we say, negative effects on career advancement. So, the following skill is preferable, even if it accomplishes less.*

First tap your first and second fingers, at the same time, on the edge of your desk.
Then tap your second and third fingers.  Repeat as fast as you can.

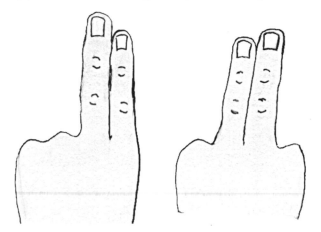

*Do this over and over until your boss asks you if you've ever considered early retirement.*

# Desk Tapping II

*...designed to prevent an overdose of excitement.*

Tap your fingers in the order shown below. The idea is: *skip a finger, go back a finger, skip a finger, go back a finger,* etc. Repeat.

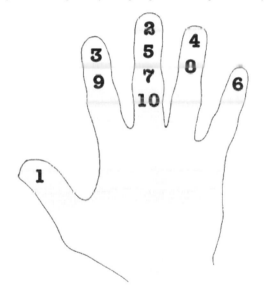

*This is also an excellent way to indicate to guest speakers just how interesting they are.*

# Desk Monster

*...not exactly what you might call a career move.*

Place these two fingers on your desk top.

Now "walk" these two fingers forward.

*Etcetera...Etcetera...ad nauseam*

# Finger Reversing

Go from this:  To this:          Or this:       To this:

Or this:          To this:

Or, for the truly insane, start like
this, and then reverse all 8 fingers.

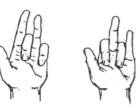

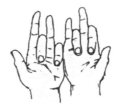

*...and be sure to get this on your next performance review.*

# Finger Splits

Follow this sequence over and over:

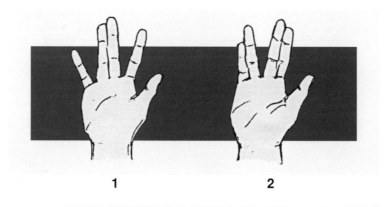

**1**          **2**

*Spock, eat your heart out.*

# This Side - That Side

Touch your 1st finger
to your pinkie, on top.

Then touch your 1st finger to your
pinkie, on bottom. And repeat.

Okay, try touching your 1st and
3rd fingers on top and bottom...

...and your 2nd finger and
pinkie, top and bottom...

 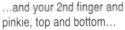

...at the same time.

*Like wiggling ears, this has nothing to do with
talent, but everything to do with useless genes.*

# Office Tap Dancing

*Do this when seated, bored, and in desperate need for attention.*

1) Toes down (on the floor), heels up.

2) Left heel down, left toe up.

3) Right heel down, right toe up.

4) Left toe down, left heel up.

5) Right toe down, right heel up.

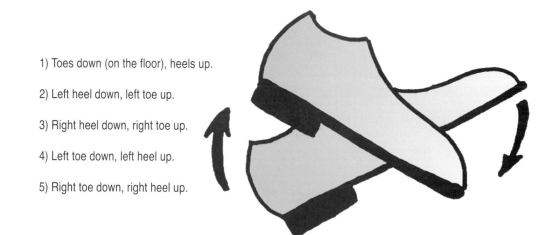

*Repeat until you get a phone call from downstairs.*

# Advanced Doodling

*Doodling is a way of putting your mind on hold. It's the brain's PAUSE button. Use it the next time you're doing nothing and the boss suddenly enters the room.*

A good doodle is like rush hour — it has no end. So, start with a theme, and then repeat.

So this…          becomes this.

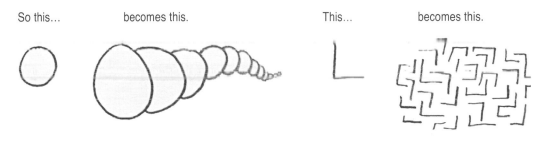

This…          becomes this.

This…          becomes this.

And this…

85

becomes this:

# How to Disappear Your Boss's Head

*...and still get that promotion.*

First try this: Close your left eye and look at the **O** with your right eye. Hold this book about 6-10 inches in front of you. Keep looking at the **O**, and *the* **X** *will seem to disappear.* If it doesn't, move the paper closer or farther away.

O                              X

Now you can do the same thing to your boss's head. The next time your boss is sitting near a wall, close your left eye and look at a spot on the wall 3-10 feet to the left of your boss's head. If you really concentrate on that spot, *your boss's head will seem to vanish.*

*...probably isn't using it anyway.*

# Necktie Magic

When you get down to it, neckties are pretty useless, unless of course you need to blow your nose. By and large, the only good thing you can say about neckties is that they give men a chance to be fashionable. But then again, considering some of the ties out there, maybe I ought to take that back. Or just take those ties back.

In any case, here's something to do with all those ties you never wear.

# Pain in the Neck

*Here's a good way to abuse yourself. Nothing compared to fluorescent lighting.*

Tie the ends of a tie together and hold it as shown. Bring your hands together and apart 3 times, saying, "One...two... *THREE!*"

On the third time, however, put your right fingers in the left loop, while simultaneously releasing your right thumb from the right loop. Keep your left thumb in its loop.

*Now PULL very fast, and if you're quick enough, your tie will appear to have penetrated your neck.*

# The Instant Knot

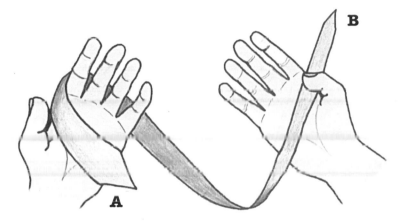

Start by holding a tie as shown. Then...

Grab **A** between the first and second fingers of right hand.
Grab **B** between the first and second fingers of left hand. Pull.

Done swiftly and smoothly, the knot appears to be tied instantaneously.

*...a good trick to know when you're late for work.*

# The Impossible Knot

*Here's an old trick that is guaranteed to annoy people. Ask your co-workers if they can tie a knot in your tie without letting go of either end.*

THE SECRET: Before picking up the tie, fold your arms, grab the ends, then unfold your arms.

*Now apply the open palm of your right hand to the middle of your forehead with sufficient force to emit the approximate sound of "THWACK."*

# The Knot from Nowhere

*You hold both ends of a necktie (preferably one that is not around your neck). Then, quicker than you can say "fax modem," an INSTANT KNOT APPEARS.*

**THE TRICK**: *Pre-tie a knot in the end of the tie, and conceal it in your right hand.* Now lift the other end to your right hand. Flick your wrist and release the end with the knot. This should look like a whipping action, which you — as an overworked office employee — are undoubtedly familiar with.

# The Knot That's Not

*This next trick is definitely useless. In fact there's only one thing that's more unproductive. A production meeting.*

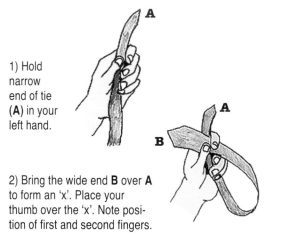

1) Hold narrow end of tie (**A**) in your left hand.

2) Bring the wide end **B** over **A** to form an 'x'. Place your thumb over the 'x'. Note position of first and second fingers.

3) Reach through the loop with your right hand. Grab **A**, and pull it a few inches back through the loop.

**THE PRESENTATION:** Tie the "knot." Hold one end in each hand. Blow on the knot while simultaneously tugging on the ends of the tie. Magic… the knot vanishes… quicker than the post-meeting stampede to the bathroom.

4) *While keeping the tie underneath your left first finger, point your left first finger at the floor. Now pull the tie all the way tight. The resulting knot looks authentic, but is actually a slip knot.*

# All Tied Up

Show this to co-workers. Almost always they will make the wrong move and get caught, but you won't because you'll know "the secret move."

Stick your right hand through this loop. Following the arrow, move your hand around the loop. Then go back through the loop from the opposite direction. When you pull, the tie will probably catch on your right arm – unless, of course, you happen to know the secret move.

**THE SECRET MOVE** (in case you were wondering): When you circle around the loop, point your right fingers *down*, not *up*, and circle the portion of the loop *below* your right arm. Done in this way, the loop slips off your arm.

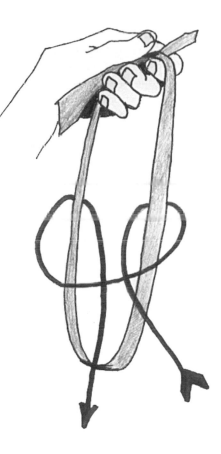

*...more useless than economic forecasting.*

# Tie Your Tie With One Hand

**1)** Starting position. (Note length of fat end.)

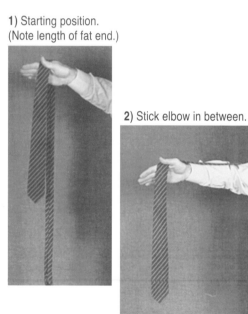

**2)** Stick elbow in between.

**3)** Grab skinny end between first and second fingers.

**4)** Straighten your arm out, allowing loop to fall off your elbow.

*...guaranteed to get you promoted – or transferred.*

# Self Abuse

Stand next to a door frame. Grab your neck or tie with your own hand and shake violently.

Now choke, gag, drool, and loudly shout any of the following:

*"What? No more coffee?"*
*"Where's my pen?!!"*
*"YOU want a RAISE?!!"*
*"You threw out WHAT?!!"*
*"What do you mean you didn't back it up?"*

# Showing Off in the Break Room

*Picture yourself in your typical break room. Hard chairs, linoleum floors, clanking candy machine, bad coffee, etc. You call this a break room? Gimme a break!*

*Of course, there's a reason why employers make break rooms so drab. It's so you won't actually take any breaks. Until now...*

# Credit Card Buzzing

Take 2 credit cards and hold them back to back so the bumpy numbers are on the outside. Hold the cards *extremely loosely* at the edge of the short sides. Now blow air between the cards. The sound you hear will precisely express your feelings about the interest you are paying.

# Coffee Cup Balancing

With practice, you can balance your coffee cup on the edge of a file.

Of course, this works better with
a little help from Mr. Thumb.

# Water Cup Twirling

*By the time you finish this page, you'll be able to twirl a full cup of water, upside down, over your head, without spilling a drop. If you dare.*

**1)** Hold a cup of water in this position. Notice your fingers are pointing away from you to the right. Does it feel awkward? Good! That means you're doing it right.

**2)** Pray that I know what I'm talking about.

**3)** Now for the moment of truth… Keeping your arm straight and your fingers pointing to the right, swing the cup in a full circle over your head and back to where you started in a *smooth, continuous and fairly fast motion.*

**4)** If Newton's laws of physics are still in effect, centrifugal force will keep the water in the cup. And you can keep your job.

# Water Cup Flipping

*Start and end with the cups nested together...*

*...or not.*

103

# Chairpeople of the Bored

*If you've been looking for a way to build team spirit, look no further.*

Set up four chairs (facing inward) and four brave souls like this:

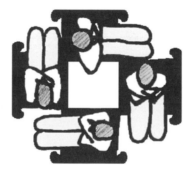

Each person lies back so that one person's shoulders rest on another person's knees. Now, you can actually remove the chairs, and your giggling friends won't fall down (in theory).

*Now for the real trick - challenge them to stand up.*

# Neck Twisting

1) Note the strategically placed plastic cup…

2) …and the sound of your friends groaning.

# Chair Pick Up

*Remember this one? Where women prove once again they are the superior (chair lifting) sex.*

**1)** Position yourself as shown, with your head against the wall, *three foot-lengths* from the wall.

**2)** Try lifting the chair and standing up.

You'll have no trouble at all – if you're a woman. But if you are a man (sorry guys), you won't be able to stand up.

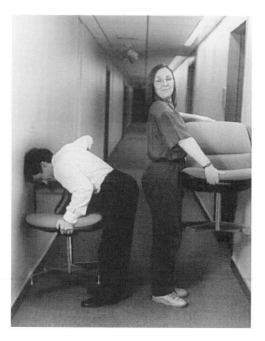

*Emasculation rears its ugly head again.*

# Office Challenges

*Commuting…interruptions…no daylight…pressure to produce. Yes, life at the office is not easy. But if office work isn't challenging enough already, here are some more activities to aggravate your day. Bet you can't…*

…sign your name while making a circle with your foot…

…crush a newspaper in one hand…

…fold a paycheck more than 7 times…

…or not think of quitting time.

I want to take this opportunity to thank you for buying (I hope) this book. Obviously, since you've chosen a book of useless office skills, you must be on the cutting edge of today's innovative, world-class, quality-minded business world. It's my sincerest hope that you have enjoyed this little training manual and have learned absolutely nothing of practical value.

Rick Davis

One answer to Disk Shuffle (from page 74):

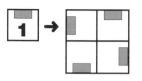

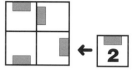

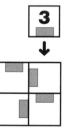

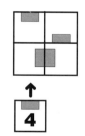

Rick Davis, *founder of the Institute of Totally Useless Skills, is a former Ringling Brothers Circus clown who has performed at DisneyWorld, on Broadway, on HBO, and at fine laundromats everywhere. He travels nationwide as a corporate comic, holds a degree in Philosophy (his first useless skill), and lives in New Hampshire with his wife and children who tolerate his compulsive, expulsive, and repulsive singing.*

Sidney Hall, Jr. *is a publisher, editor, columnist, teacher, and poet; in other words, a jackass of all trades. He is a Phi Beta Kappa graduate of Reed College where he earned a totally useless degree in Greek and Latin Classics. His poetry has appeared in numerous journals and magazines. His first book of poems,* What We Will Give Each Other, *has been highly acclaimed. He lives in New Hampshire with his wife, two children, and compost pile.*

# **M**ore from the Institute of Totally Useless Skills...

### **The Video.** The oddest training video ever! Pencil Tricks…Letter Opener Swallowing…Phone Songs…Calculator Words… Briefcase Balancing…Rubber Band Stunts…Business Card Tricks…The Best Paper Airplane…Paper Clip Diversions…Credit Card Buzzing. Great for meeting breaks. *25 minutes. VHS. $19.95 plus $4 shipping & handling. Call 1-800-345-6665.*

### **Live Presentations.** Comic speeches and workshops by Rick Davis. Guaranteed to lighten things up at the office, to be the entertainment hit of your business year, and to provide absolutely nothing of practical value. *Contact A.E.I. Speakers Bureau, 1-800-44SPEAK.*

### **The Web Site.** A new useless office skill every day! Print it out and post it on your bulletin board, in your company newsletter, or under your puppy.

### **www.jlc.net/~useless**

### *ORDER BOOKS AND VIDEOS BY PHONE, FAX, OR E-MAIL*

1-800-345-6665
FAX: 603-357-2073
E-mail: pbs@top.monad.net

# ...And more from Hobblebush Books

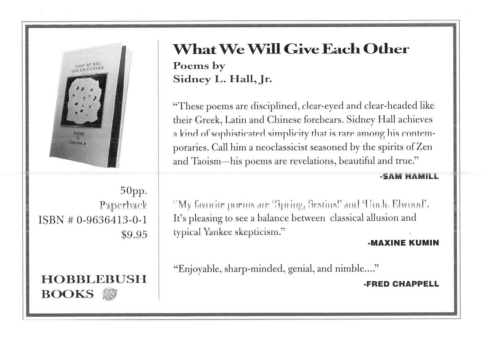

**What We Will Give Each Other**
**Poems by**
**Sidney L. Hall, Jr.**

"These poems are disciplined, clear-eyed and clear-headed like their Greek, Latin and Chinese forebears. Sidney Hall achieves a kind of sophisticated simplicity that is rare among his contemporaries. Call him a neoclassicist seasoned by the spirits of Zen and Taoism—his poems are revelations, beautiful and true."

**-SAM HAMILL**

"My favorite poems are 'Spring, Restius' and 'Uncle Elwood'. It's pleasing to see a balance between classical allusion and typical Yankee skepticism."

**-MAXINE KUMIN**

"Enjoyable, sharp-minded, genial, and nimble...."

**-FRED CHAPPELL**

50pp.
Paperback
ISBN # 0-9636413-0-1
$9.95

**HOBBLEBUSH
BOOKS**

## *GREAT GIFTS!*

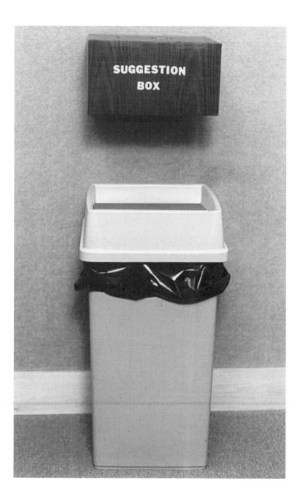